BEST AUSTRALIAN
POLITICAL CARTOONS
2015

RUSS RADCLIFFE created the annual Best Australian Political Cartoons series in 2003. In 2007, he produced *Man of Steel: a cartoon history of the Howard Years*, and in 2013, *Dirt Files: a decade of Best Australian Political Cartoons*. He has edited collections from some of Australia's finest political cartoonists, including Alan Moir, Bruce Petty, Bill Leak, Matt Golding, and Judy Horacek.

'I'm determined to learn from all of this.'
— Tony Abbott, prime minister

BEST AUSTRALIAN POLITICAL CARTOONS
2015

edited by
Russ Radcliffe

SCRIBE
Melbourne · London

Scribe Publications
18–20 Edward St, Brunswick, Victoria 3056, Australia
2 John St, Clerkenwell, London, WC1N 2ES, United Kingdom

First published by Scribe 2015

Copyright © this selection Russ Radcliffe 2015
Individual cartoons copyright © contributing cartoonists 2015

All rights reserved. Without limiting the rights under copyright reserved above, no part of this publication may be reproduced, stored in or introduced into a retrieval system, or transmitted, in any form or by any means (electronic, mechanical, photocopying, recording or otherwise) without the prior written permission of the publishers of this book.

Typeset in Veljovic 10/14 pt

Printed and bound in Australia by Ligare

A Cataloguing-in-Publication record for this title is available from the National Library of Australia

9781925106978 (pbk)

scribepublications.com.au
scribepublications.co.uk

Front cover image: Alan Moir, *Sydney Morning Herald*
Back cover image: David Pope, *The Canberra Times*

Commissioned
and produced by

www.highhorse.com.au
russ@highhorse.com.au

Cartoonists

Dean Alston	31, 41, 56, 65, 135, 183	Peter Lewis	54, 95, 155
		Eric Löbbecke	vi, 19, 62, 180
Peter Broelman	20, 27, 30, 49, 83	Reg Lynch	2, 11, 94, 158
Pat Campbell	2, 63, 84, 133, 159, 178	Alan Moir	iii, 3, 36, 64, 81, 96, 104, 107, 118, 123, 142, 185
Oslo Davis	55		
Chris Downes	10, 15, 92, 181	Peter Nicholson	136, 160
Andrew Dyson	8, 22, 70, 88, 121, 122, 147, 153	Bruce Petty	1, 25, 43, 58, 91, 98, 131, 139, 148
Anton Emdin	40, 46	David Pope	3, 4, 7, 50, 52, 68, 90, 102, 130, 143, 152, 169
John Farmer	69, 124, 167		
First Dog on the Moon	12, 26, 29, 59, 120, 156	Geoff Pryor	48, 105, 117, 129, 154, 170, 176
Lindsay Foyle	172		
Matt Golding	28, 33, 34, 42, 72, 79, 150, 174	David Rowe	5, 44, 76, 82, 97, 113, 119, 126, 146, 161, 186
Judy Horacek	86, 93, 101, 110		
Fiona Katauskas	16, 38, 51, 132	Greg Smith	32, 35, 106
Mark Knight	6, 9, 39, 71, 73, 100, 168, 175	John Spooner	18, 37, 77, 80, 89, 112, 115, 128, 138
Jon Kudelka	23, 53, 57, 61, 75, 114, 127, 134, 162, 179	Ron Tandberg	21, 74, 85, 99, 116, 171
		Jos Valdman	45
Sean Leahy	60, 164, 177	Andrew Weldon	14, 141, 163
Bill Leak	4, 17, 47, 108, 125, 137, 140, 149, 166	Cathy Wilcox	24, 67, 87, 103, 111, 145, 151, 157, 182
Glen Le Lievre	13, 78, 109, 144, 184	Paul Zanetti	66, 165, 173

Eric Löbbecke
The Australian

'When I've been up close to these things, not only are they visually awful, but they make a lot of noise.'
— Tony Abbott

Introduction

The switch from total warrior to nation builder is a hard road — just ask Tony Abbott's political hero, Winston Churchill. A 'better stopper than starter' (p. 23), many pundits predicted Abbott would not be up to the kinds of negotiations and consensus building that effective government requires. But few suspected how rapidly these failings would destroy his leadership. Abbott's rapid and permanent collapse in the polls was a brutal indication of how little love the public had for him and his agenda. The realisation of Malcolm Turnbull's 'brilliant career' (Moir p. 185) had seemed inevitable all year.

If the voting public had, out of exasperation at Labor's chaos, reluctantly put aside their suspicions about Abbott's harder ideological agenda and chose to believe the soporific 'no surprises' promise he made during the 2013 election campaign, they were in for a shock.

Joe Hockey's first budget, in 2014, an austerity program that was meant to signal an end to the culture of 'entitlement', was hugely unpopular, and morphed into a disastrous bonfire of the coalition's political capital. The government was forced to spend much of its energy in the following year trying to recover.

The incompetently sold budget, Abbott's continued adherence to an expensive paid parental-leave scheme, his failure to listen and consult, and a particular anger directed at his autocratic chief of staff, Peta Credlin, suggested that the coalition's problems were more fundamental than a few troublesome barnacles on an otherwise smooth-sailing ship of state (p. 6). The simmering backbench discontent suggested that Abbott himself was the biggest barnacle (p. 7). But it was his captain's call in knighting Prince Philip — likened to a drunken rugby-tour moment by Lynch (p. 11) — that transformed what might have been dismissed as a storm in a teacup (p. 8) into a tsunami of ridicule, which almost destroyed his leadership

Promising that he would change, Abbott survived his near-death experience (p. 22)

and, in a disconcerting echo of Gillard's reference to a 'good government which lost its way', promised that 'good government starts today'.

By mid-year, things had stabilised, and murmurings from the backbench — despite Credlin's continued presence — were hushed. Countering his harsh and 'unfair' first budget, Hockey's second was promised to be 'dull and boring'. (p. 61) The rhetoric of austerity and emergency was abandoned, and the can of reform (p. 62) was kicked down the road in favour of what looked suspiciously like pre-election giveaways. An early poll was on everyone's mind, and Abbott appeared confident, energised, and in full campaign mode.

But things didn't go exactly to plan. Even on national security, the coalition's favoured territory, the attempt to wedge Labor as a party that was 'rolling out the red carpet to terrorists' was rendered ineffective by Bill Shorten's lockstep support of anti-terror legislation.

Indeed, challenges to the proposal to revoke the citizenship of dual nationals fighting for proscribed organisations were more rigorously dissected by members of the cabinet than by the opposition (p. 128). Highly detailed and damaging leaks highlighted the serious internecine split between the small 'l' liberal and conservatives, who continued their arguments in the media. Public disagreement over marriage equality reinforced the impression that a fractious coalition was tearing itself apart.

And then there was Bronwyn. The intense pressure on Bill Shorten following his testimony at the Royal Commission into Trade Union Governance and Corruption was relieved by the debate about Bronwyn Bishop's fitness to remain as Speaker of the House (p. 166). Abbott's loyalty to Bishop merely extended the pain and media scrutiny. The legitimacy of the commission itself and any of its findings was then called into question by revelations about the relationship of the head of the commission, Dyson Heydon, with the Liberal Party.

Meanwhile, despite this supposedly being its 'year of ideas', Labor kept its head down and locked in behind the government in the politically dangerous areas of national and border security.

Shorten's biggest battle of the year was with his own party. In a high-stakes move intended to remove the political wedge of asylum-seeker policy, so effectively deployed by the coalition against Labor since Tampa, Shorten admitted Labor's past 'mistakes' and meekly accepted the efficacy of boat turnbacks (p. 164). It was an act of contrition or betrayal, depending on your point of view, but the left was forced to acquiesce, and Shorten's authority in the party was considerably strengthened.

Malcolm Turnbull defeat of Abbott has radically changed the game. If the new prime minister can appease the conservative wing of the coalition and contain their desire for retribution, and suppress his own imperious tendencies — big 'ifs' — he will be a formidable opponent. Slipping into the Lodge in the shadow of Abbott's unpopularity is no longer an option for Labor; they have every reason to be nervous.

The year 2015 opened with the murder by self-proclaimed Islamist extremists of 11 cartoonists, writers, and staff of French satirical magazine *Charlie Hebdo* for publishing offensive cartoons depicting the Prophet. Any doubts about the real-world implications of political cartooning were instantly dispelled (pp. 34–7).

To the satirical mind schooled in the rich, and subversive traditions of the Enlightenment, religion has always provided a target-rich environment, and *Charlie*'s cartoonists have never pulled their punches on either bishops or imams.

It is the nature of satire that it must offend. If no one is upset, it is just light comedy. The best satirists are, at some level, pissed off at the state of the world, and they direct their anger at the perceived source of the problem. In this respect, satire and hate-speech are uncomfortable bedfellows. When PEN elected to grant

its annual Freedom of Expression award to *Charlie Hebdo* in the wake of the murders, 26 members protested, believing that *Charlie* had rolled onto the wrong side of that particular bed. They argued that principled support for free expression didn't necessarily extend to enthusiastic approval for gratuitous offence. The debate settled into a well-worn binary, bounded by a kind of free-speech absolutism on one side and an apologetic cultural relativism on the other.

It's certainly not the job of political cartoonists to be ambassadors for multiculturalism, or for any other 'worthy' cause. But their unspoken contract licenses them to offend in order to reveal a deeper truth behind the manipulated appearances of public life. Freedom of expression occurs in a context, and it is naive to characterise the effects of *Charlie Hebdo*'s cartoons on France's alienated Muslim minorities as simply collateral damage in a just war. While fanaticism was firmly in their frame, their targeting was, at times, loose. That shouldn't have been a capital crime. Whatever the arguments about the quality or wisdom of *Charlie Hebdo*'s cartoons, no one deserves to be murdered for their ideas.

Atena Farghadani, an Iranian cartoonist, chose her targets with great seriousness, precision, and intent. Without a hint of the gratuitous, she depicted Iran's politicians and mullahs as monkeys and cows. For offending their autocratic sensibilities, she was jailed for 12 years.

As David Pope says, 'Here's to the freedom to draw monkeys and cows.'
Russ Radcliffe

David Rowe
The Australian Financial Review

'Before Christmas, and even after Christmas, if Tony had come up into my area he'd have been as popular as a floater in a swimming pool.'
— Warren Entsch

Mark Knight
Herald Sun

'There are one or two barnacles still on the ship but by Christmas they will have been dealt with.'
— Tony Abbott

David Pope
The Canberra Times

'Howard used to talk about knocking off barnacles when 80 per cent of things were good and the 20 per cent needed fixing. This government has 80 per cent wrong.'
— former John Howard power-broker

Andrew Dyson
The Age

'Abbott again. Tough to write, but if he won't replace top aide Peta Credlin she must do her patriotic duty and resign.'
— Rupert Murdoch

Mark Knight
Herald Sun

'She doesn't seem to trust Tony by himself. She goes to every meeting with him, she attends every function. She seems to worry about what he might do if left to his own devices.'
— Coalition frontbencher, anon.

Christopher Downes
The Mercury

'If you're so stupid and so dopey as this prime minister and his ministerial team are, you can expect anything.'
 — Doug Cameron

Reg Lynch
The Sun-Herald

'He didn't really knight a prince, did he?'
— Terri Butler

First Dog on the Moon
The Guardian

Glen Le Lievre
The Sun-Herald

'As the country has grown stronger, its politics have become nastier and more adolescent.'
— Nick Bryant, BBC correspondent in Australia

Andrew Weldon
The Sunday Age

Christopher Downes
The Mercury

'Why are you still on the frontbench?'
— Bill Shorten to Malcolm Turnbull

Fiona Katauskas
New Matilda

Bill Leak
The Australian

'They are like two Siamese fighting fish stuck in the same tank.'
— Coalition frontbencher, anon.

John Spooner
The Age

'To be the leader of a political party you only need one attribute and that is to have the confidence of the party room ... He is the best person because he has the confidence of the party room.'
— Malcolm Turnbull

Eric Löbbecke
The Australian

'We think that when you elect a government, when you elect a prime minister, you deserve to keep that government and that prime minister until you have a chance to change your mind.'
— Tony Abbott

Peter Broelman
www.broelman.com.au

'My question is to the prime minister: Given that one-third of her parliamentary colleagues and a quarter of her cabinet colleagues have today expressed their lack of confidence in her, how can she claim to have a mandate to continue as prime minister?'
— Tony Abbott, Opposition leader, 2012

Ron Tandberg
The Age

'Given that nearly half of his parliamentary colleagues, including two-thirds of his Liberal backbenchers, have today expressed a lack of confidence in the prime minister, how can the prime minister claim to have a mandate for this country?'
— Bill Shorten, Opposition leader, 2015

Andrew Dyson
The Age

'On the night before the last election, the prime minister promised: No cuts to education, no cuts to health, no change to pensions, no change to the GST and no cuts to the ABC or SBS. Is the prime minister regarded as box office poison in Victoria because he is breaking every single one of these promises?'
— Bill Shorten

'I'm a fighter. I know how to beat Labor Party leaders. I beat Kevin Rudd, I beat Julia Gillard, I can beat Bill Shorten as well. What I'm not good at is fighting the Liberal Party.'

— Tony Abbott

Cathy Wilcox
The Sun-Herald

'Let's stop the navel gazing, let's forget the internals and let's get on with governing the country.'

— Tony Abbott

Bruce Petty
The Age

'He's a very intelligent, courageous, brave man, a very thoughtful guy. He's got a wonderful self-deprecating sense of humour.'
— Malcolm Turnbull

First Dog on the Moon
The Guardian

'You cannot help but feel cynical about the timing of these raids, the fact that it is whipping people up into a frenzy of hysteria, or war fever.'
— Randa Abdel-Fattah, writer

Matt Golding
The Sunday Age

'You know we are all part of team Australia ... and you are our captain.'
— Muslim community leader to Tony Abbott

First Dog on the Moon
The Guardian

Peter Broelman
www.broelman.com.au

'Anyone who supports sharia law in Australia should not have the right to vote, should not be given government handouts and should probably pack up their bags and get out of here.'
— Jacqui Lambie

Dean Alston
The West Australian

'We are pushing them back into their homes, we're pushing them away from society that we want them to be part of.'
— Maha Abdo, Muslim Women's Association

Greg Smith
The Sunday Times

'The jihadi threat is real but many Australians also see Abbott as a terror as he takes a wrecking ball to our social infrastructure.'
— Alannah MacTiernan

Matt Golding
The Sunday Age

'Those people who attack Muslims and Islam in Australia are doing precisely what ISIL wants. Now, more than ever, we need to stand up for our tolerant, multicultural society. Racial and religious vilification is totally unacceptable.'
— Malcolm Turnbull

Matt Golding
The Sunday Age

'The *Charlie Hebdo* killers are best seen as the armed wing of the Empire of Offence, the horrific logical conclusion to the institution of a new era of speech-punishing inoffensiveness.'
— Brendan O'Neill

Greg Smith
The Sunday Times

'The magazine [*Charlie Hebdo*] seems to be entirely sincere in its anarchic expressions of disdain toward organised religion. But in an unequal society, equal opportunity offense does not have an equal effect.'
— 26 writers, including Peter Carey, oppose PEN award for *Charlie Hebdo*

Alan Moir
The Sydney Morning Herald

'By punching downward, by attacking a powerless, disenfranchised minority with crude, vulgar drawings closer to graffiti than cartoons, *Charlie* [*Hebdo*] wandered into the realm of hate speech.'
— Garry Trudeau, creator of *Doonesbury*

John Spooner
The Age

'I've since had the feeling that, if the attacks against *The Satanic Verses* had taken place today, these people would not have defended me, and would have used the same arguments against me, accusing me of insulting an ethnic and cultural minority.'
— Salman Rushdie, writer

Fiona Katauskas
New Matilda

Mark Knight
Herald Sun

'In the days when I was a journalist there were no metadata protections for journalists and if any agency, including the RSPCA or the local council, had wanted my metadata, they could have just gone and got it on authorisation. Look, I was perfectly comfortable as a journalist.'

— Tony Abbott, on his journalistic experience in the 1980s

Anton Emdin
The Spectator Australia

'Look, I'm going to shirtfront Mr Putin. You bet I am. I am going to be saying to Mr Putin Australians were murdered. They were murdered by Russian-backed rebels using Russian-supplied equipment.'
— Tony Abbott

Dean Alston
The West Australian

'I would advise Russia's President Vladimir Putin to wash his hands carefully and sterilise them after shaking the paw offered to him by Australia's prime minister Tony Abbott at the forthcoming G20 summit in Brisbane.'

— Timothy Bancroft-Hinchey, *Pravda* columnist

Matt Golding
The Sunday Age

'This was Tony Abbott's moment in front of the most important and influential leaders in the world and he's whingeing that Australians don't want his GP tax.'
— Bill Shorten

Bruce Petty
The Age

'It beggars belief that Tony Abbott made a fool of himself, boasting about abolishing an emissions trading scheme in front of a room of people who are committed to taking action on global warming.'
— Christine Milne

David Rowe
The Australian Financial Review

'Submarines are the spaceships of the ocean.'
— John Madigan

Jos Valdman
The Advertiser

'They're $350 million over budget on three Air Warfare Destroyer builds ... You wonder why I wouldn't trust them to build a canoe?'
— David Johnston on the Australian Submarine Corporation

Anton Emdin
The Spectator Australia

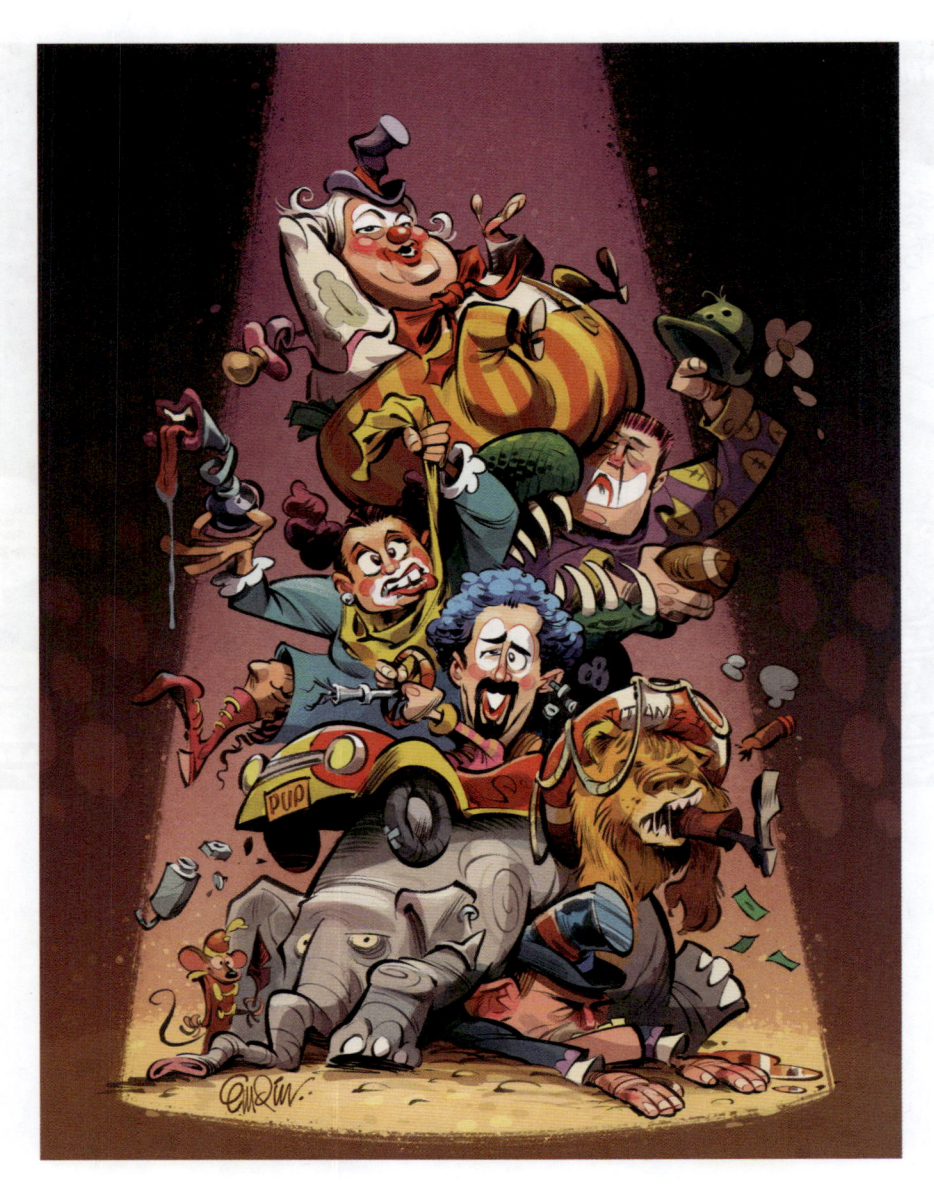

Bill Leak
The Australian

'China must be aware that Palmer's rampant rascality serves as a symbol that Australian society has an unfriendly attitude toward China.'
— *The Global Times*

Geoff Pryor
The Saturday Paper

'When you start a new party like our party the established parties and others try to wreck it. She's been sent in there by someone to cause trouble and I think that's the reality of it.'
— Clive Palmer.

Peter Broelman
www.broelman.com.au

'Glenn Lazarus does not know what it is like to be on a proper team.'
— Clive Palmer

David Pope
The Canberra Times

'It's not a combat mission, but Iraq is a dangerous place … and I can't tell you that this is risk-free.'
— Tony Abbott

Fiona Katauskas
New Matilda

'This is not a distant crisis for us, it is absolutely in our national interest that ISIL be defeated.'
— Bill Shorten

David Pope
The Canberra Times

'It was completely unacceptable for Indonesia to proceed as it did when critical legal processes were yet to run their course, raising serious questions about Indonesia's commitment to the rule of law.'
— Tony Abbott

'If Canberra keeps doing things that displease Indonesia, Jakarta will surely let the illegal immigrants go to Australia. There are more than 10,000 in Indonesia today. If they are let go to Australia, it will be like a human tsunami.'
— Tedjo Edhy Purdijatno, Indonesian government minister

Peter Lewis
Newcastle Herald

"RELAX JOHNNO, A HUNDRED YEARS FROM NOW WHO'S GUNNA CARE?"

'Lest we forget, Anzac 1915–2015.
Fresh in our Memories.'
— Woolworths ad

Oslo Davis
The Age

Dean Alston
The West Australian

'This is already the vastest war in history. It is a war not of nations, but of mankind. It is a war to exorcise a world-madness and end an age ... For this is now a war for peace. It aims straight at disarmament. It aims at a settlement that shall stop this sort of thing for ever. Every soldier who fights against Germany now is a crusader against war. This, the greatest of all wars, is not just another war — it is the last war!'
— H.G. Wells, August 1914

Jon Kudelka
www.kudelka.com.au

'I would suggest that people stop looking back to what it was and focus on the challenges of today and tomorrow, no matter who they are.'
— Joe Hockey

Bruce Petty
The Age

'The only reason I agreed to do it is because I was told that it would be independent, bipartisan and non-political ... If it turns out to have been fiddled with or subject to political interference from one side of politics I would deeply regret playing any part in it whatsoever.'
— Dr Karl Kruszelnicki, Intergenerational Report advertising campaign

First Dog on the Moon
The Guardian

Sean Leahy
The Courier Mail

'The more fundamental problem the 2014–2015 budget faced was that the public was not persuaded tough measures were necessary in the first place.'
— Malcolm Turnbull

'This budget certainly will be much less exciting than last year's budget because the task this year is at least 50 per cent reduced from this task last year.'
— Tony Abbott

Eric Löbbecke
The Australian

'We will need a decade of unprecedented policy action by government, and leadership and risk-taking by business ... Our politicians across all parties have to prepare the community for the enormous social and economic change that must take place in our society.'

— Jennifer Westacott, Business Council of Australia

Pat Campbell
The Canberra Times

'When the government released its discussion paper on tax it said "lower, simpler, fairer". Ever since we have been flooded with demands for taxes that are higher, more complicated and less economic. "Lower, simpler, fairer" is looking like a morbid joke.'
— Peter Costello

Alan Moir
The Sydney Morning Herald

'People said, "Oh $20,000, you know, what can you do with $20,000?" Well, I was watching television, I had a few moments off last night, and I was watching *Downton Abbey* and they've dropped the price of a ute to under $20,000 so that the tradies of our country can take advantage of the instant asset write-off.'
— Tony Abbott

Dean Alston
The West Australian

'This budget is last year's budget repackaged for an opinion poll.'
— Bill Shorten

Paul Zanetti
www.zanetti.net.au

'With our current budget constraints, the better focus now is on childcare if we want higher participation and a stronger economy. So a bigger, better paid parental leave scheme is off the table.'
— Tony Abbott

Cathy Wilcox
The Sun-Herald

'This Government doesn't support double dipping. We don't support double dipping. And what those opposite, Madam Speaker, have made very clear, is that they do and they designed the system for double dipping.'
— Scott Morrison

David Pope
The Canberra Times

'Too many politicians are too concerned about being liked rather than getting things done.'
— Sophie Mirabella

John Farmer
The Mercury

'This budget is last year's meanness wrapped up in new trickery.'
— Bill Shorten

Andrew Dyson
The Age

'Christopher Pyne is embarrassing himself and needs to stop harassing me and other crossbenchers.'
— Glenn Lazarus

Mark Knight
Herald Sun

'There has been a lack of preparation and consultation before such a fundamental change to Australia's higher education policy.'
— Nick Xenophon

Matt Golding
The Sunday Age

'There's nothing malevolent about Joe, he's a good bloke; but his preferred mode of debate is stream-of-consciousness.'
— Liberal MP, anon.

Mark Knight
Herald Sun

'I stand by my Treasurer. I stand by my team.'
— Tony Abbott

Ron Tandberg
The Age

'It may well be the case that people are coming back into the workforce at the age of 80.'
— Joe Hockey

Jon Kudelka
www.kudelka.com.au

'I would fully expect within over the [next] 10-year period, there will be a downturn for some reason of some depth. The question is: can we be in a position to do the things that would make it a shallow and short one?'
— Glenn Stevens, Reserve Bank of Australia governor

David Rowe
The Australian Financial Review

'When you look at the housing price bubble evidence, it's unequivocally the case in Sydney, unequivocally.'
— John Fraser, treasury secretary

John Spooner
The Age

'The starting point for a first home buyer is to get a good job that pays good money.'
— Joe Hockey

Glen Le Lievre
The Sun-Herald

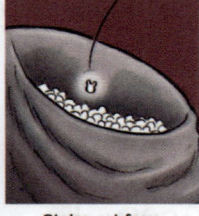

'The Australian Tax Office needs to be prepared to name and shame the worst offenders. Frankly, if you're prepared to engage in these kinds of tax minimisation practices, you should be prepared to front it publicly and justify it to the Australian community.'
— Sam Dastyari, Senate tax inquiry

Matt Golding
The Sunday Age

'Are you serious? You've come to this inquiry on tax minimisation and aggressive tax minimisation and you weren't expecting a question like that? So $6 billion, you can't tell us how much of that's gone overseas?'
— Nick Xenophon, Senate tax inquiry

John Spooner
The Age

'Anti-trade activists who are trying to derail negotiations for the world's largest regional trade and investment deal are effectively trying to stop Australian agriculture from surging ahead.'
— Andrew Robb

Alan Moir
The Sydney Morning Herald

'Any defence co-operation between countries should not harm the interests of the third country.'
— Hong Lei, Chinese Foreign Ministry, on US–Australia military ties

David Rowe
The Australian Financial Review

'Yesterday's decision on the Liverpool Plains is definitely a tick in the positive box in relation to reconsidering re-entering the fray in terms of politics ... This piece of land they are talking about, and it's not about coal versus no coal, it's about water and how it relates to agriculture.'

— Tony Windsor

'The land we stand on is intrinsic to our values and identity as a nation. I wouldn't want to see Australian farmland become under the control of the government of another nation.'

— Barnaby Joyce

Pat Campbell
The Canberra Times

'We have to work until we have every policeman, every magistrate, every judge understanding the complexities of family violence. I will not stop until that happens.'
— Rosie Batty, Australian of the Year 2015

Ron Tandberg
The Age

> CARDINAL PELL HAS DEFENDED THE ACTIONS OF ARCHBISHOP PELL AND DOES NOT WISH TO BE HELD ACCOUNTABLE FOR THE BEHAVIOUR OF FATHER PELL

'I would also like Cardinal George Pell to publicly acknowledge that child sexual abuse was committed by clergy and Brothers under his watch as the parish priest in Ballarat East. I would like him to apologise for this.'
— witness, Royal Commission into Institutional Responses to Child Sexual Abuse

Judy Horacek
www.horacek.com.au

Cathy Wilcox
The Sun-Herald

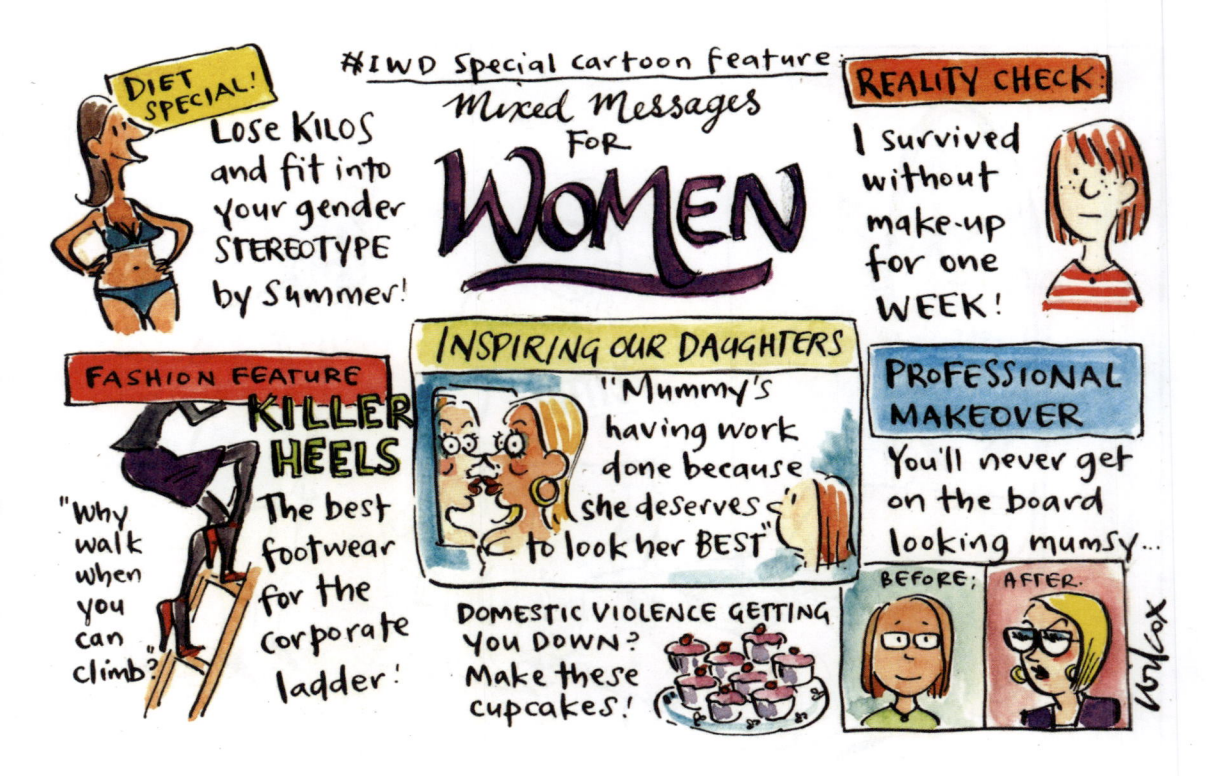

'The Liberal National Party will host its International Women's Day event at a men's only club in Brisbane. As the Minister for Women, does the prime minister think this is right?'
— Bill Shorten

Andrew Dyson
The Age

'In less than three years an astonishing reform agenda leapt off the policy platform and into legislation and the machinery and programs of government. The country would change forever. The modern cosmopolitan Australia finally emerged like a technicolour butterfly from its long dormant chrysalis.'
— Noel Pearson, Cape York Institute

John Spooner
The Age

'Dying will happen sometime. As you know, I plan for the ages, not just for this life.'
— Gough Whitlam

David Pope
The Canberra Times

'The full quotation is, "Life's not meant to be easy, but take courage, child, for it can be delightful".'

— Malcolm Fraser

Bruce Petty
The Age

'Nope, nope, nope.'
— Tony Abbott

Christopher Downes
The Mercury

'Do you know what the meaning of hopeless and helpless is? Do you know what is the meaning of I got tired of being alive?'
— open letter from Nauru detainee

Judy Horacek
www.horacek.com.au

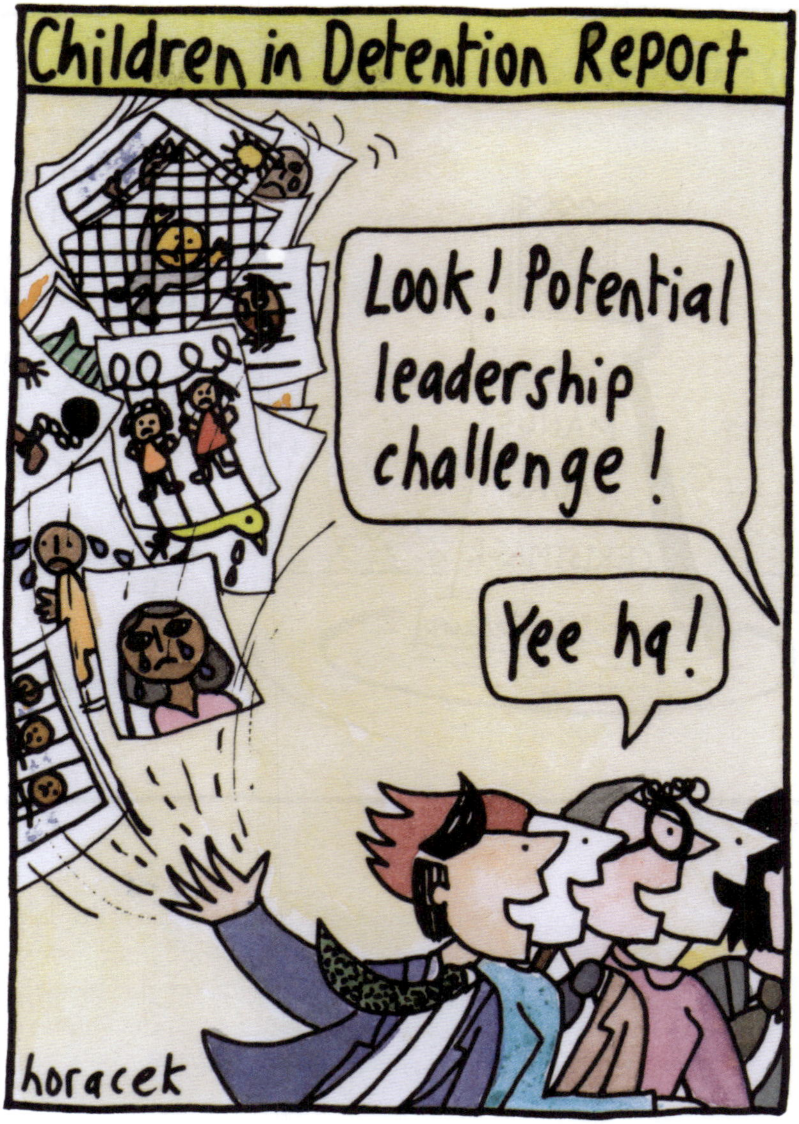

Reg Lynch
The Sun-Herald

'Just as we've looked back on the white Australia policy, I have no doubt that my grandchildren and their children will look back at this period in our history and think "what did they think they were doing and how did they allow themselves to demean Australia and themselves in that way?" ... I believe that will be the verdict of history.'
— Jon Stanhope, outgoing Christmas Island administrator

Peter Lewis
Newcastle Herald

'Well there would be no self harm in the centre if they hadn't gotten on a leaky boat and paid thousands of dollars to be there ... You can't deny that that's the truth.'
— Barry Hasse, incoming Christmas Island administrator

Alan Moir
The Sydney Morning Herald

'It's absolutely crystal clear this inquiry by the president of the Human Rights Commission is a political stitch-up. All I know, Madam Speaker, is that this government has lost confidence in the president of the Human Rights Commission.'
— Tony Abbott

David Rowe
The Australian Financial Review

'I'm not sure whether the prime minister's presiding over it or whether he's orchestrating it but [it appears to be] a campaign to denigrate, debilitate and I think possibly destabilise or even destroy an independent commission.'
— Brian Burdekin, former federal human rights commissioner

Bruce Petty
The Age

'Have we thought about what the consequences are of pushing people back to our neighbour Indonesia? Is it any wonder that Indonesia will not engage with us on other issues that we care about, like the death penalty?'
— Gillian Triggs, Human Rights Commission president

Ron Tandberg
The Age

'It's an international embarrassment, and it's an embarrassment for all Australians that we would have someone in a public office making comments like this that are completely unfounded.'
— Peter Dutton

Mark Knight
Herald Sun

'Australians are like British people but with balls of steel, can-do brains, tiny hearts and whacking great gunships. Their approach to migrant boats is the sort of approach we need in the Med.'
— Katie Hopkins, columnist, *The Sun* UK

Judy Horacek
www.horacek.com.au

David Pope
The Canberra Times

'We are not about litigating or prosecuting against those who would wish to disclose issues and as I mentioned earlier, whistleblower protection laws are quite robust in this country.'
— Roman Quaedvlieg, Australian Border Force

Cathy Wilcox
The Sun-Herald

'This law is designed to do one thing — that is prevent scrutiny by the media, by the community, and in fact by the world, of Australia's detention centres and the shame of those detention centres.'
— Greg Barns, barrister

Alan Moir
The Sydney Morning Herald

'What we do is stop the boats by hook or by crook, because that's what we've got to do and that's what we've successfully done.'
— Tony Abbott

Geoff Pryor
The Saturday Paper

'Wow, a state bribing, that certainly doesn't fit with the correct ethics in state relations.'
— Jusuf Kalla, Indonesian vice president

Greg Smith
The Sunday Times

'Leaders must act. Time is not on our side ... Please reduce your investments in the coal- and fossil fuel-based economy and [move] to renewable energy.'
— Ban Ki-moon, United Nations secretary general

Alan Moir
The Sydney Morning Herald

'Let's have no demonisation of coal. Coal is good for humanity, coal is good for prosperity, coal is an essential part of our economic future, here in Australia, and right around the world.'
— Tony Abbott

Bill Leak
The Australian

'This is the first time in the history of mankind that we are setting ourselves the task of intentionally, within a defined period of time, to change the economic development model that has been reigning for at least 150 years, since the industrial revolution.'
— Christiana Figueres, United Nations Framework Convention on Climate Change

Glen Le Lievre
The Sun-Herald

♪ "It's not easy bein' green..." ♪

'Figueres is on record saying democracy is a poor political system for fighting global warming. Communist China, she says, is the best model. This is not about facts or logic. It's about a new world order under the control of the United Nations.'
— Maurice Newman, Prime Minister's Business Advisory Council chair

Judy Horacek
www.horacek.com.au

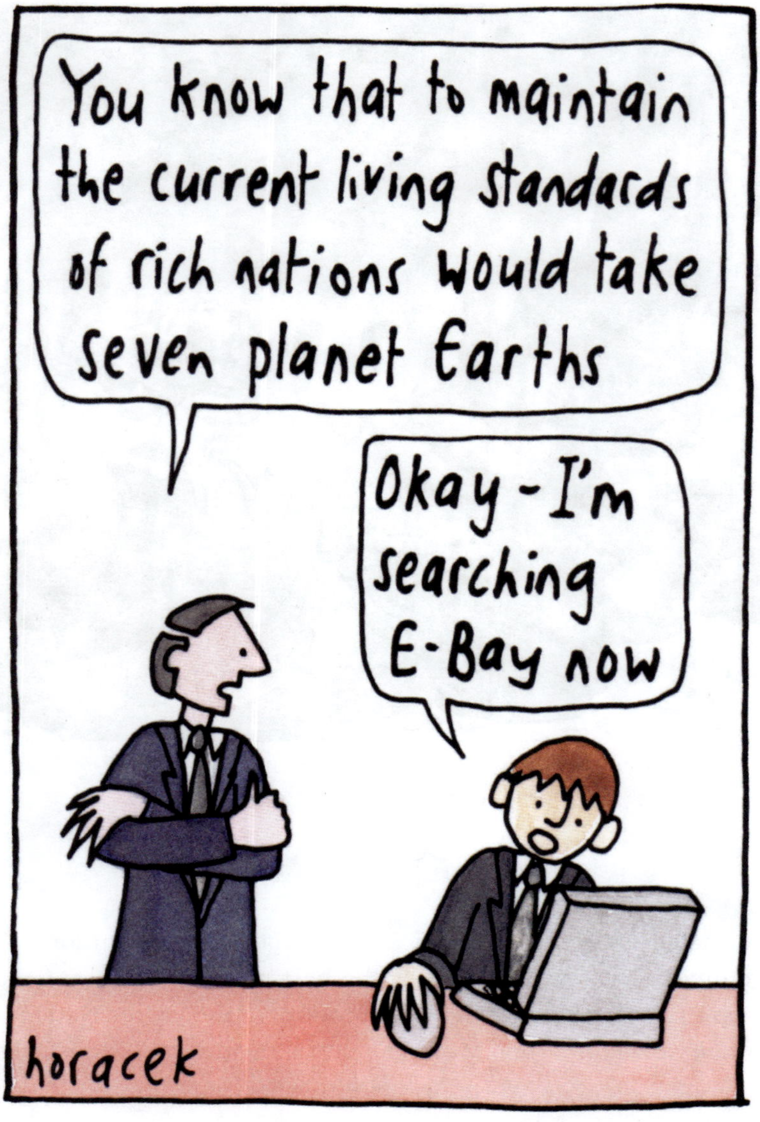

Cathy Wilcox
The Sun-Herald

'With one of the world's highest levels of per capita emissions, Australia has gone from leadership to free-rider status in climate diplomacy.'
— Kofi Annan, former secretary general of the United Nations

John Spooner
The Age

'If present trends continue, this century may well witness extraordinary climate change and an unprecedented destruction of ecosystems, with serious consequences for all of us.'
— Pope Francis

David Rowe
The Australian Financial Review

'This seems to be another suspect captain's pick by someone trying to provide sponsorship for a fellow climate change warrior whose academic standards are highly questionable.'

— Alannah MacTiernan on Bjorn Lomborg's Australian Consensus Centre at the University of Western Australia

Jon Kudelka
www.kudelka.com.au

'This is more than a joke. Tony Abbott is actively campaigning against an industry that employs thousands of Australians, attracts billions in investment, and reduces Australia's carbon pollution.'
— Mark Butler

John Spooner
The Age

'Frankly it's right and proper we've reduced the Renewable Energy Target because as things stood there was going to be an explosion of these things right around our country. There will still be some growth but it will be much less than it would otherwise have been thanks to measures this government has taken.'
— Tony Abbott

Ron Tandberg
The Age

'We have been living in our own little bubble, and you can't live in your own little bubble forever.'
— Ross Garnaut, economist

Geoff Pryor
The Saturday Paper

..SANS CULOTTES...

'I think if world leaders like Barack Obama can make time in their schedule to attend then Tony Abbott should also attend.'
— Mark Butler on the 2015 United Nations Climate Change Conference, Paris

Alan Moir
The Sydney Morning Herald

'I think we're the natural home for people who've got progressive mainstream values.'
— Richard Di Natale, new Greens leader

David Rowe
The Australian Financial Review

'Does it really matter who will lead the freedom-hating Greens?'
— Kevin Andrews

First Dog on the Moon
The Guardian

Andrew Dyson
The Age

'A person's citizenship is of enormous importance, intrinsic to themselves. Take me. The only people who've lived in Australia longer than my family are Aboriginal. I have no other identity. Are we seriously saying some minister could take my citizenship?'
— Malcolm Turnbull

Andrew Dyson
The Age

'We've got to keep our country safe. We are going to keep terrorists out where they're dual nationals and it seems the Opposition wants to bring them home. No doubt roll out the red carpet for them like it rolled out the red carpet for people smugglers when it was in government.'
— Tony Abbott

Alan Moir
The Sydney Morning Herald

'The very interesting thing this morning is Mr Dreyfus's bombshell that the Labor party is not going to support stopping terrorists from coming back to our country. I think Australians would be amazed by that ... I don't want these people coming back to our country ... having been taught how to make bombs, cut people's heads off.'
— Peter Dutton

John Farmer
The Mercury

'We know, instinctively, that anyone who raises a gun or a knife to an Australian because of who we are has utterly forfeited any right to be considered one of us. That is what we believe. What do you believe? Do you want dual-national citizens to keep their citizenship?

— Tony Abbott

Bill Leak
The Australian

'Here we go again. Talking about something as momentous as this and there is nothing in front of us. There's a discussion paper that only a few of us have seen. This is a shambles.'
— Malcolm Turnbull

David Rowe
The Australian Financial Review

'In the end, if people can't abide by the confidentially of the cabinet room they should leave the cabinet ... Where it becomes apparent, the prime minister has made clear he is going to take action.'
— Ian Macfarlane

Jon Kudelka
www.kudelka.com.au

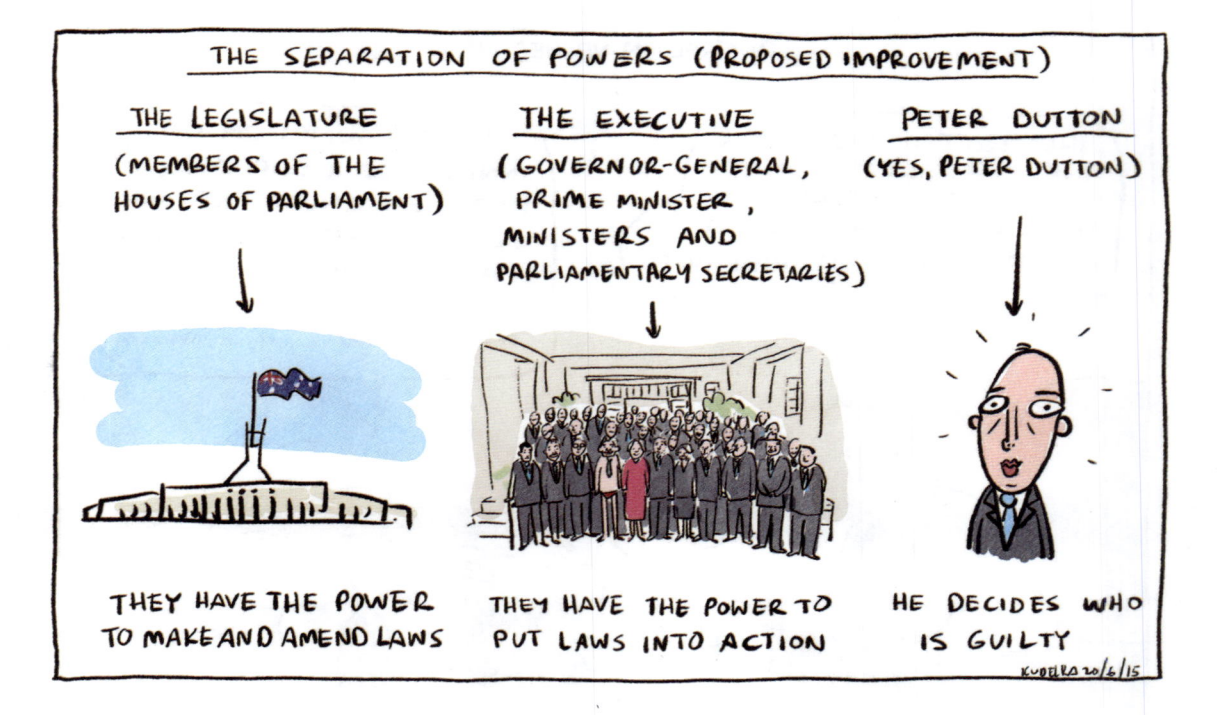

THE SEPARATION OF POWERS (PROPOSED IMPROVEMENT)

THE LEGISLATURE (MEMBERS OF THE HOUSES OF PARLIAMENT)
↓
THEY HAVE THE POWER TO MAKE AND AMEND LAWS

THE EXECUTIVE (GOVERNOR-GENERAL, PRIME MINISTER, MINISTERS AND PARLIAMENTARY SECRETARIES)
↓
THEY HAVE THE POWER TO PUT LAWS INTO ACTION

PETER DUTTON (YES, PETER DUTTON)
↓
HE DECIDES WHO IS GUILTY

Barnaby Joyce: If you don't have enough evidence to charge them in a court, how can you have enough evidence to take away their citizenship?
Peter Dutton: That's the point, Barnaby. You don't need too much evidence. It's an administrative decision.
  — leaked notes from Cabinet meeting

John Spooner
The Age

'I am the Attorney-General. It is my job to stand for the rule of law.'
— George Brandis

Geoff Pryor
The Saturday Paper

'It's not good enough that laws simply be tough, this is not a sort of bravado issue, they've got to be the right laws, you've got to get the measure right.'
— Malcolm Turnbull

David Pope
The Canberra Times

'Q: Why should this power be exercised by a minister and not the courts?
A: A law requiring a terrorist conviction would be toothless.'
— leaked Coalition Question Time brief

Bruce Petty
The Age

'Over the last 15 years or so, the major political parties have agreed with each other to pass laws that threaten some of the most fundamental rights and freedoms that we have inherited from our common law tradition.'
— Gillian Triggs, Human Rights Commission president

Fiona Katauskas
New Matilda

'2014 was defined by the force of Labor's resistance. Today I commit to you that Labor will be defined in 2015 by the power of our ideas.'
— Bill Shorten

Pat Campbell
The Canberra Times

'What we won't be doing is playing the small target opposition. We won't be rolling into a little ball. This is a marathon, not a sprint ... We won't be backwards in coming forwards with ideas and policies.'
— Chris Bowen

Jon Kudelka
www.kudelka.com.au

'We can't sit back and hope that the cruel cuts of Liberal governments will deliver us an electoral dividend. We need to offer a positive alternative vision.'
— Bill Shorten

Dean Alston
The West Australian

'If he stood up and argued for something significant, Shorten might find voters warming to him as a man of conviction. Currently they regard him as a non-event.'
— Mark Latham

Peter Nicholson
The Australian

Bill Leak
The Australian

'I understand that voters have not given me a mandate against Europe, but a mandate for a sustainable solution.'
— Alexis Tsipras, Greek prime minister

John Spooner
The Age

'Iran is led by suicidal, apocalypse-seeking, America-hating, Israel-denying theocratic fanatics. If these ayatollahs have nuclear weapons, they will use them, someday, somewhere. Iran is a major, longtime state sponsor of terrorism; its leaders are entirely bereft of restraint, decency and respect for human life.'
— Mitt Romney

Bruce Petty
The Age

'If Congress kills this deal, we will lose more than just constraints on Iran's nuclear program or the sanctions we have painstakingly built. We will have lost something more precious: America's credibility as a leader of diplomacy. America's credibility as the anchor of the international system.'
— Barack Obama

Bill Leak
The Australian

'We think our politics is pretty brutal, but I have to say, your politics makes ours look positively genteel.'
— Phillip Hammond, British foreign secretary

Andrew Weldon
The Sunday Age

Alan Moir
The Sydney Morning Herald

'Hillary Clinton was the worst Secretary of State in the history of the United States. There's never been a Secretary of State so bad as Hillary. The world blew up around us. We lost everything, including all relationships. There wasn't one good thing that came out of that administration or her being Secretary of State.'
— Donald Trump, US presidential candidate, 2016

David Pope
The Canberra Times

'It's all entertainment. I think he's having the time of his life, being up on that stage, saying whatever he wants to say.'
— Hillary Clinton, US presidential candidate, 2016

Glen Le Lievre
The Sun-Herald

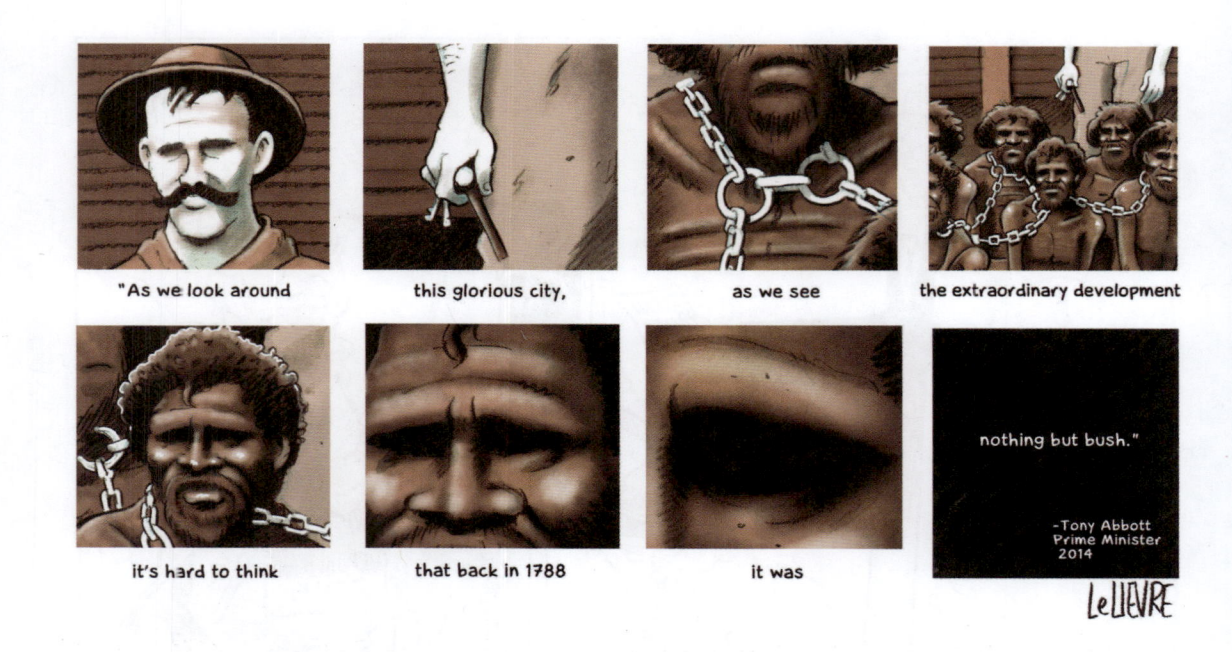

"As we look around this glorious city, as we see the extraordinary development it's hard to think that back in 1788 it was nothing but bush."

-Tony Abbott
Prime Minister
2014

'As we look around this glorious city, as we see the extraordinary development, it's hard to think that back in 1788 it was nothing but bush, and that the Marines and the convicts and the sailors that struggled off those twelve ships, just a few hundred yards from where we are, must have thought they'd come almost to the Moon.'
— Tony Abbott

Cathy Wilcox
The Sun-Herald

'Well it was a defining moment, there's no argument about that. It was also a disastrous defining moment for Indigenous people.'
— Warren Mundine, Prime Minister's Indigenous Advisory Council chair

David Rowe
The Australian Financial Review

'What we can't do is endlessly subsidise lifestyle choices if those lifestyle choices are not conducive to the kind of full participation in Australian society that everyone should have.'
— Tony Abbott

Andrew Dyson
The Age

'There was time in our history when they kicked us out of town, they kicked us out of town and now they want to bring us back in just by a flick of the policy switch.'
— Noel Pearson, Cape York Institute

Bruce Petty
The Age

'Recognition of the first peoples in the Constitution sends a message that you are valued, you are important, that we want to respect you, and we want to deal with the things that have caused us division and discord in the past.'
— Patrick Dodson, Yawuru man

Bill Leak
The Australian

'I would have preferred to stay in Cape York at my beach house, with my kids, and sent a cardboard cut-out down to this meeting today. It was very beautifully finessed, might I say. Both [the prime minister and the Opposition leader] did a very good job of pretending to listen, I thought.'

— Noel Pearson, Cape York Institute

Matt Golding
The Sunday Age

'This isn't a WA thing or an AFL thing — it's an Australian issue. To be called an Abo, a nigger, a black so-and-so, for your entire life, and then expected to sit there and accept it, it's a reflection on Australia and where we are as a country.'
— Michael O'Loughlin, retired Swans AFL player

Cathy Wilcox
The Sun-Herald

'The man is always a victim. Then he became Australian of the Year and tells us that we're all racists; every time he speaks, Australia is a racist nation.'
— Alan Jones, broadcaster, on Adam Goodes

David Pope
The Canberra Times

'I'm happy to look you straight in the eye and say that I'd be pleased to be part of a government that would say you are out of the country, as far as I'm concerned. I would sleep very soundly at night with that point of view.'
— Steve Ciobo

Andrew Dyson
The Age

'Now, frankly, heads should roll over this. Heads should roll over this.'
— Tony Abbott

Geoff Pryor
The Saturday Paper

'I do think the ABC needs to have a long hard look at itself, and answer a question I've posed before: whose side are you on?'
— Tony Abbott

Peter Lewis
Newcastle Herald

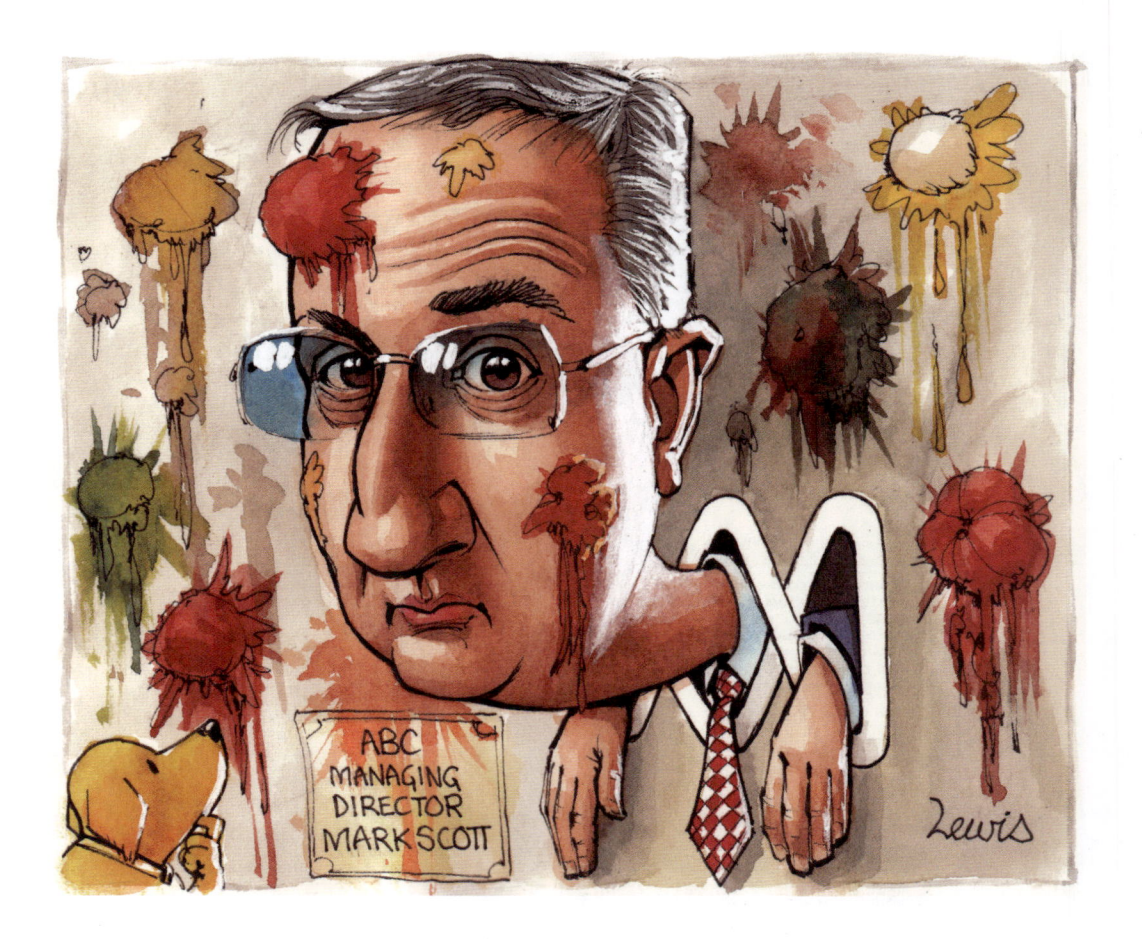

'The A in ABC is for Australian. And the part we play, what we do for the side, is a vital one, central to our culture and our democracy — that of being an independent public broadcaster.'

— Mark Scott, Australian Broadcasting Corporation managing director

First Dog on the Moon
The Guardian

Cathy Wilcox
The Sun-Herald

THE NEW TERROR ALERT SYSTEM

BEFORE	NOW	WHAT IT MEANS
LOW	NOT EXPECTED	We're polling well
MEDIUM	POSSIBLE	Labor just announced a popular policy
HIGH	PROBABLE	Overseas incident — Bronwyn's overspent again
EXTREME	EXPECTED	We're tanking in the polls
	CERTAIN	OK this is real now.

'Unfortunately, there are some people in the Labor Party who don't take national security as seriously as they should.'
— Tony Abbott

Reg Lynch
The Sun-Herald

'I want to say publicly thank you to the ABC. Thank you to the ABC. I don't normally say thank you to the ABC, but I have to say Australia is indebted to you on this instance.'
— Tony Abbott, on *The Killing Season*

Pat Campbell
The Canberra Times

'How is it possible that you win an election in November 2007, on the scale that you do, with the goodwill that you have, with the permission that you are gifted by the public, and you manage to lose all that goodwill, to trash the permission and to find yourself out of office within just six years ... No one can escape blame for that in my view.'
— Alan Milburn, British Labour politician

Peter Nicholson
The Australian

'I've got to say it's the first time that I've seen a union official grilled for not being sufficiently militant at a royal commission.'
— Greg Combet

David Rowe
The Australian Financial Review

'What we've seen here is the Americanisation of Australian politics, where incumbents use these kinds of processes, "show trials", to smear political opponents.'
— Sam Dastyari

Jon Kudelka
www.kudelka.com.au

'Dear Bill, is the concept of conflict of interest beyond your understanding? ... Bill, do something for the ALP. It's simple. Just go.'
— Bob Hogg, former Labor national secretary

Andrew Weldon
The Sunday Age

Sean Leahy
The Courier Mail

'I can no longer escape the conclusion that Labor, if we form a government, needs to have all the options on the table. It's not easy, though, because it involves the admission, I think, that mistakes were made when Labor was last in government.'
— Bill Shorten

Paul Zanetti
www.zanetti.net.au

'I do think there will be a lot of people this morning asking whether they will be able to vote for Labor.'
— Anna Burke

Bill Leak
The Australian

'If Mr Abbott does not repudiate the actions of his captain's pick, the Speaker of the Parliament, then he is effectively endorsing a view which says that — that they are so important that they don't even have to drive on the same roads as the rest of Australians.'
— Bill Shorten

John Farmer
The Mercury

'It was Bronwyn's decision, the helicopter was her call. She didn't have to get a helicopter to Geelong, that's what set this thing off.'
— Malcolm Turnbull

Mark Knight
Herald Sun

'Bronwyn Bishop is not a fit person to occupy the highest position in the House of Representatives. The Member for Mackellar has abused parliamentary entitlements and treats public expectations with contempt. No wonder many members of the community question her integrity.'
— Andrew Wilkie

David Pope
The Canberra Times

'I would call on all my colleagues ... to stand firm against the demands of the Labor Party to remove the Speaker. This is the Labor Party that ... removed two prime ministers because they couldn't take the pressure poured on them by the media or the Opposition at the time, so let's not repeat the mistakes of our opponents by jumping at the first whiff of grapeshot.'
— Christopher Pyne

Geoff Pryor
The Saturday Paper

'She has been a strong Speaker … she has been a strong servant of our country, she has been a good servant of the Coalition and so she does have my confidence, but like everyone who has done something like this, inevitably, for a period of time, they are on probation.'
— Tony Abbott

Ron Tandberg
The Age

'Goodbye Bronwyn. Bronwyn, goodbye. Goodbye Bronwyn! Bronwyn, Bronwyn, Bronwyn. Goodbye, bye, bye. Goodbye Bronwyn. Bronwyn, goodbye. Goodbye. Twittley-too.'
— Clive Palmer

Lindsay Foyle
New Matilda

'What had become apparent, particularly over the last few days, is that the problem is not any particular individual — the problem is the entitlements system more generally.'
— Tony Abbott

Paul Zanetti
www.zanetti.net.au

'The Age of Entitlement should never have been allowed to become a fiscal nightmare. But now that it has, governments around the world must reign in their excesses and learn to live within their means. All of our futures depend on it.'
— Joe Hockey, 2012

Matt Golding
The Sunday Age

'I would think that if I was a gay activist, people would say "Oh, just another bloody fairy out there trying to push his own agenda", but because of my background, people are a little bit puzzled by it and sitting up and listening ... and in fact I'm getting a lot of people that are not gay coming up to me and saying to me "Hey, you know, we've got gay friends and family too".'

— Warren Entsch, on his same-sex marriage private members bill

Mark Knight
Herald Sun

'This is indicative of Shorten's broader political problem. He only takes on issues that are easy: flimflam such as gay marriage, Indigenous constitutional recognition and the republic.'
— Mark Latham

Geoff Pryor
The Saturday Paper

'Tony Abbott is a man who will fight tooth and nail to be yesterday's man. We saw that he is prepared to use every tactic in order to block progress. And we saw that he is prepared to tear his own party apart in order to get his own way.'
— Penny Wong

Sean Leahy
The Courier Mail

'Are we in the Asian century or not? It's amazing how certain people try to pick and choose in relation to debates. All of the sudden the United States, which is usually condemned, is now being celebrated on this bizarre decision of a 5–4 decision in the Supreme Court.'
— Eric Abetz

Pat Campbell
The Canberra Times

'Lots of homosexuals don't want to get married. Dolce & Gabbana never got married.'
— attributed to Eric Abetz

'This is a destruction of marriage, not simply a redefinition.'
— Kevin Andrews

Eric Löbbecke
The Australian

'He said it was Cabinet that was causing most of the trouble. He senses the mood of the backbench, which is angry over the public fights.'
— Cabinet minister, anon.

Christopher Downes
The Mercury

'If somebody is gutless and in breach of the rules one really wonders why a journalist even bothers to repeat comments from such an individual.'
— Eric Abetz

Cathy Wilcox
The Sun-Herald

'A leader should not lie — to their colleagues or the Australian people. The truth is often difficult, but any political figure who looks the public in the eye and betrays their trust is not worthy of office.'
— Teresa Gambaro

Dean Alston
The West Australian

'I think Australians are just utterly sick of federal politics and I'm not surprised why. They are poisoning the well of goodwill for all other elected politicians in the country.'
— Matthew Guy, Victorian Opposition leader

Glen Le Lievre
The Sun-Herald

'This is a government defined by disappointment, deceit and incompetence. The opposition leader who promised so much has morphed into a confused prime minister — a man rapidly sinking into the quicksand of his own negativity.'
— Anthony Albanese

Alan Moir
The Sydney Morning Herald

'Now if we continue with Mr Abbott as prime minister, it is clear enough what will happen. He will cease to be prime minister and he'll be succeeded by Mr Shorten.'
— Malcolm Turnbull

David Rowe
Australian Financial Review

'I firmly believe that our party is better than this, that our government is better than this and, by God, that our country is so much better than this.'
— Tony Abbott